MW00962220

Place a picture of
yourself in front of the
EPCOT ball here.

THIS BOOKS BELONGS TO:

TABLE OF CONTENTS

copyright © 2016 D Magical Education All Rights

MEXICO

Modeled after an ancient, mexican, Aztec temple, the building at the Mexico pavilion is breathtaking. Full of intricate details, it is a work of art in itself. The temple houses a "twilight village" inside, along with artifacts from Mexico and a Mayan calendar. Be sure to watch the Mayan calendar for a while, as it changes colors over a period of time.

MEXICO PAVILION OPENED OCTOBER 1, 1982

CAN YOU NAME THE 31 STATES OF MEXICO?

ASK A KIDCOT CAST MEMBER TO WRITE YOUR NAME OR A SPECIAL MESSAGE (IN SPANISH) IN THE BOX BELOW, THEN STAMP THE SMALLER SQUARE.

3

copyright © 2016 D Magical Education. All Rights Reserved

MEXICO

Méjico (me'-hi-ko)

LIST YOUR 5 FAVORITE THINGS ABOUT THE MEXICO PAVILION:

1. _____

2. _____

3. _____

4. _____

5. _____

FLAG OF MEXICO

CAPITAL	Mexico City
LANGUAGE	Spanish
MONEY	Pesos
PEOPLE	Mexicans
CONTINENT	North America

copyright © 2016 D Magical Education All Rights

MEXICO

The outfits that each cast member wear, reflects their home country. How does the outfit for the Mexico pavilion cast members stand-out? If you need help, ask a cast member!

_____

_____

_____

_____

TRY **2** DIFFERENT FOODS FROM THE MEXICO PAVILION. RATE HOW YOU LIKE THEM.

I tried: _____

Liked it?
circle one

Why? _____

I tried: _____

Liked it?
circle one

Why? _____

Find some authentic candy from Mexico at the pavilion. Try it. Did you notice the writing on the wrappers? What does the writing mean in your language? Keep the empty candy wrappers and attach them here.

5

copyright © 2016 D Magical Education. All Rights Reserved

NORWAY

The Gol stavkirke, or stave church located at the Norway pavilion, is a replica of a church, built in 1212 A.D., now located in Hallingdal, Norway. Inside this medieval marvel, you will find many different artifacts such as model ships, folk art, clothing, musical instruments and more, based on the culture of Norway, which was the inspiration for the Disney movie, Frozen.

CAN YOU NAME THE 5 REGIONS OF NORWAY?

ASK A KIDCOT CAST MEMBER TO WRITE YOUR NAME OR A SPECIAL MESSAGE (IN NORWEGIAN) IN THE BOX BELOW, THEN STAMP THE SMALLER SQUARE.

NORWAY PAVILION
OPENED JUNE 3, 1988

copyright © 2016 D Magical Education All Rights

Norge (NAHR-i-geh)

NORWAY

FLAG OF NORWAY

CAPITAL	Oslo
LANGUAGE	Norsk
MONEY	Norwegian Krone
PEOPLE	Norwegians
CONTINENT	Europe

LIST YOUR 5 FAVORITE THINGS ABOUT THE NORWAY PAVILION:

1. _____

2. _____

3. _____

4. _____

5. _____

7

copyright © 2016 D Magical Education All Rights Reserved

NORWAY

Find some authentic candy from Norway at the pavilion. Try it. Did you notice the writing on the wrappers? What does the writing mean in your language? Keep the empty candy wrappers and attach them here.

TRY 2 DIFFERENT FOODS FROM THE NORWAY PAVILION. RATE HOW YOU LIKE THEM.

I tried: _____

Liked it?
circle one

Why? _____

_____

I tried: _____

Liked it?
circle one

Why? _____

The outfits that each cast member wear, reflects their home country. How does the outfit for the Norway pavilion cast members stand-out? If you need help, ask a cast member!

_____

_____

_____

_____

_____

copyright © 2016 D Magical Education All Rights

CHINA

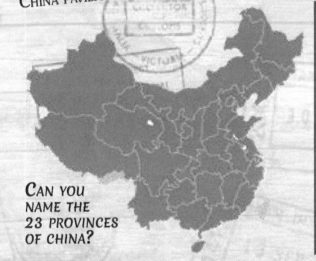

CHINA PAVILION OPENED OCTOBER 1, 1982

As you step through the Paifang Gate, into the China pavilion, you will see a magnificent marble entranceway to the Temple of Heaven replica, modeled after the original in Beijing, China. The temple is full of cultural artifacts and traditional items from China. Don't forget to watch the "Reflections of China" presentation for a glimpse into the Chinese culture.

ASK A KIDCOT CAST MEMBER TO WRITE YOUR NAME OR A SPECIAL MESSAGE (IN CHINESE) IN THE BOX BELOW, THEN STAMP THE SMALLER SQUARE.

CAN YOU NAME THE 23 PROVINCES OF CHINA?

9

copyright © 2016 D Magical Education All Rights Reserved

CHINA

中国 (Zhōng-guó)

LIST YOUR 5 FAVORITE THINGS ABOUT THE CHINA PAVILION:

1. _____

2. _____

3. _____

4. _____

5. _____

FLAG OF CHINA

CAPITAL	Beijing
LANGUAGE	Chinese/Mandarin
MONEY	Yuan
PEOPLE	Chinese
CONTINENT	Asia

copyright © 2016 D Magical Education All Rights

CHINA

The outfits that each cast member wear, reflects their home country. How does the outfit for the China pavilion cast members stand-out? If you need help, ask a cast member!

_____

_____

_____

_____

TRY 2 DIFFERENT FOODS FROM THE CHINA PAVILION. RATE HOW YOU LIKE THEM.

I tried: _____

Liked it?
circle one

Why? _____

I tried: _____

Liked it?
circle one

Why? _____

Find some authentic candy from China at the pavilion. Try it. Did you notice the writing on the wrappers? What does the writing mean in your language? Keep the empty candy wrappers and attach them here.

11

copyright © 2016 D Magical Education All Rights Reserved

GERMANY

Decorated with a statue of St. George and the Dragon in the middle, and a clock tower with a large cuckoo clock at the rear, the Platz (square) is located at the back of the Germany pavilion. Each building around the Platz is designed to look like buildings in a German town from different times and regions of Germany, with a Bavarian flair. Don't forget to check out the model train village at the edge of the pavilion.

GERMANY PAVILION
OPENED JUNE 3, 1988

ASK A KIDCOT CAST MEMBER TO WRITE YOUR NAME OR A SPECIAL MESSAGE (IN GERMAN) IN THE BOX BELOW, THEN STAMP THE SMALLER SQUARE.

CAN YOU NAME THE 16 STATES OF GERMANY?

copyright © 2016 D Magical Education All Rights

Deutschland (d-oy-tsch-lund)   GERMANY

FLAG OF GERMANY

CAPITAL	Berlin
LANGUAGE	German
MONEY	Euros
PEOPLE	Germans
CONTINENT	Europe

LIST YOUR 5 FAVORITE THINGS ABOUT THE GERMANY PAVILION:

1. _____

2. _____

3. _____

4. _____

5. _____

13

copyright © 2016 D Magical Education. All Rights Reserved

GERMANY

Find some authentic candy from Germany at the pavilion. Try it. Did you notice the writing on the wrappers? What does the writing mean in your language? Keep the empty candy wrappers and attach them here.

TRY 2 DIFFERENT FOODS FROM THE GERMANY PAVILION. RATE HOW YOU LIKE THEM.

I tried: _____

Liked it?
circle one

Why? _____

I tried: _____

Liked it?
circle one

Why? _____

The outfits that each cast member wear, reflects their home country. How does the outfit for the Germany pavilion cast members stand-out? If you need help, ask a cast member!

_____

_____

_____

_____

_____

copyright © 2016 D Magical Education All Rights

ITALY

ITALY PAVILION
OPENED OCTOBER 1, 1982

CAN YOU NAME THE 20 REGIONS OF ITALY?

As you enter the Italy pavilion, an 83 foot tall campanile (bell tower) sits on your left. It was designed as a mirror image of the original campanile in St. Mark's Square at Venice. The replica of Doge's Palace (Palazzo Ducale), a 14th century palace turned museum sits at the towers base. Be sure to check out the gondolas tied up in the World Showcase lagoon.

ASK A KIDCOT CAST MEMBER TO WRITE YOUR NAME OR A SPECIAL MESSAGE (IN ITALIAN) IN THE BOX BELOW, THEN STAMP THE SMALLER SQUARE.

copyright © 2016 D Magical Education All Rights Reserved

ITALY

Italia (iy-TAALYaa)

LIST YOUR **5** FAVORITE THINGS ABOUT THE ITALY PAVILION:

1. _____

2. _____

3. _____

4. _____

5. _____

FLAG OF ITALY

CAPITAL	Rome
LANGUAGE	Italian
MONEY	Euros
PEOPLE	Italians
CONTINENT	Europe

copyright © 2016 D Magical Education All Rights

ITALY

The outfits that each cast member wear, reflects their home country. How does the outfit for the Italy pavilion cast members stand-out? If you need help, ask a cast member!

_____

_____

_____

_____

_____

TRY 2 DIFFERENT FOODS FROM THE ITALY PAVILION. RATE HOW YOU LIKE THEM.

I tried: _____

Liked it?
circle one

Why? _____

I tried: _____

Liked it?
circle one

Why? _____

Find some authentic candy from Italy at the pavilion. Try it. Did you notice the writing on the wrappers? What does the writing mean in your language? Keep the empty candy wrappers and attach them here.

copyright © 2016 D Magical Education All Rights Reserved

AMERICA

At the center of the America pavilion is the American Adventure building. It took 5 years to build! The architecture features several famous buildings from the revolutionary time period of the 1700's, including former president Thomas Jefferson's Monticello. Inside the stately building is a theater that shows monumental events in America's history.

AMERICA PAVILION
OPENED OCTOBER 1, 1982

ASK A KIDCOT CAST MEMBER TO WRITE YOUR NAME OR A SPECIAL MESSAGE (IN ENGLISH) IN THE BOX BELOW, THEN STAMP THE SMALLER SQUARE.

CAN YOU NAME THE 50 STATES OF AMERICA?

copyright © 2016 D Magical Education All Rights

America

AMERICA

FLAG OF AMERICA

CAPITAL	Washington D.C.
LANGUAGE	English
MONEY	Dollar
PEOPLE	Americans
CONTINENT	North America

LIST YOUR 5 FAVORITE THINGS ABOUT THE AMERICA PAVILION:

1. _____

2. _____

3. _____

4. _____

5. _____

copyright © 2016 D Magical Education. All Rights Reserved

AMERICA

Find some authentic candy from America at the pavilion. Try it. Did you notice the writing on the wrappers? What does the writing mean in your language? Keep the empty candy wrappers and attach them here.

TRY **2** DIFFERENT FOODS FROM THE AMERICA PAVILION. RATE HOW YOU LIKE THEM.

I tried: _____

Liked it?
circle one

Why? _____

I tried: _____

Liked it?
circle one

Why? _____

The outfits that each cast member wear, reflects their home country. How does the outfit for the America pavilion cast members stand-out? If you need help, ask a cast member!

_____

_____

_____

_____

_____

copyright © 2016 D Magical Education All Rights

JAPAN

At the edge of the World Showcase lagoon, a Torii gate sits, welcoming visitors the the Japan pavilion. It is modeled after the Torii gate just off the coast of Itsukushima Island in southern Japan. At the actual entrance to the pavilion, sits a five story Japanese pagoda, which is a replica of the 7th century Horyuji Temple in Ikaruga, Japan.

JAPAN PAVILION
OPENED OCTOBER 1, 1982

CAN YOU NAME THE **8** REGIONS OF JAPAN?

ASK A KIDCOT CAST MEMBER TO WRITE YOUR NAME OR A SPECIAL MESSAGE (IN JAPANESE) IN THE BOX BELOW, THEN STAMP THE SMALLER SQUARE.

copyright © 2016 D Magical Education. All Rights Reserved.

JAPAN

日本 (Ni-hon)

LIST YOUR **5** FAVORITE THINGS
ABOUT THE JAPAN PAVILION:

1. _____

2. _____

3. _____

4. _____

5. _____

FLAG OF JAPAN

CAPITAL	Tokyo
LANGUAGE	Japanese
MONEY	Yen
PEOPLE	Japanese
CONTINENT	Asia

copyright © 2016 D Magical Education All Rights

JAPAN

The outfits that each cast member wear, reflects their home country. How does the outfit for the Japan pavilion cast members stand-out? If you need help, ask a cast member!

_____

_____

_____

TRY 2 DIFFERENT FOODS FROM THE JAPAN PAVILION. RATE HOW YOU LIKE THEM.

I tried: _____

Liked it?
circle one

Why? _____

I tried: _____

Liked it?
circle one

Why? _____

Find some authentic candy from Japan at the pavilion. Try it. Did you notice the writing on the wrappers? What does the writing mean in your language? Keep the empty candy wrappers and attach them here.

copyright © 2016 D Magical Education. All Rights Reserved

MOROCCO

When you enter the Morocco pavilion, you are entering a city in Morocco. This city features a Minaret (tower), a Fes House (typical house in Morocco), and a replica of Bab Boujeloud, the gateway to the Fez medina. Each of these buildings is an archetectural feat, built by Moroccan artisians sent by King Hasan II. Be sure to check out the many Moroccan mosiacs on display.

MOROCCO PAVILION OPENED
SEPTEMBER 7, 1984

ASK A KIDCOT CAST MEMBER TO WRITE YOUR NAME OR A SPECIAL MESSAGE (IN ARABIC) IN THE BOX BELOW, THEN STAMP THE SMALLER SQUARE.

CAN YOU NAME THE 12 REGIONS OF MOROCCO?

copyright © 2016 D Magical Education All Rights

المغرب (Al Maghrib)

MOROCCO

FLAG OF MOROCCO

CAPITAL	Rabat
LANGUAGE	Classical Arabic
MONEY	Dirham
PEOPLE	Moroccans
CONTINENT	Africa

LIST YOUR 5 FAVORITE THINGS ABOUT THE MOROCCO PAVILION:

1. _____

2. _____

3. _____

4. _____

5. _____

copyright © 2016 D Magical Education. All Rights Reserved

MOROCCO

Find some authentic candy from Morocco at the pavilion. Try it. Did you notice the writing on the wrappers? What does the writing mean in your language? Keep the empty candy wrappers and attach them here.

TRY 2 DIFFERENT FOODS FROM THE MOROCCO PAVILION. RATE HOW YOU LIKE THEM.

I tried: _____

Liked it?
circle one

Why? _____

I tried: _____

Liked it?
circle one

Why? _____

The outfits that each cast member wear, reflects their home country. How does the outfit for the Morocco pavilion cast members stand-out? If you need help, ask a cast member!

_____

_____

_____

_____

copyright © 2016 D Magical Education All Rights

FRANCE

Welcome to a neighborhood in France! Spanning the bridge into the International Gateway, to the Monsieur Paul restaurant, the France pavilion encompasses French street artists, marble fountains, perfume shops and Les Halles Boulangerie and Patisserie (food and bakery markets). In the distance, the Eiffel Tower stands tall as the symbol of France.

FRANCE PAVILION OPENED OCTOBER 1, 1982

CAN YOU NAME THE 13 REGIONS OF FRANCE?

ASK A KIDCOT CAST MEMBER TO WRITE YOUR NAME OR A SPECIAL MESSAGE (IN FRENCH) IN THE BOX BELOW, THEN STAMP THE SMALLER SQUARE.

27

copyright © 2016 D Magical Education All Rights Reserved

FRANCE

France (Fr-h-awn-se)

LIST YOUR 5 FAVORITE THINGS ABOUT THE FRANCE PAVILION:

1. _____

2. _____

3. _____

4. _____

5. _____

FLAG OF FRANCE

CAPITAL	Paris
LANGUAGE	French
MONEY	Euros
PEOPLE	French
CONTINENT	Europe

copyright © 2016 D Magical Education All Rights

FRANCE

The outfits that each cast member wear, reflects their home country. How does the outfit for the France pavilion cast members stand-out? If you need help, ask a cast member!

_____

_____

_____

_____

TRY 2 DIFFERENT FOODS FROM THE FRANCE PAVILION. RATE HOW YOU LIKE THEM.

I tried: _____

Liked it?
circle one

Why? _____

I tried: _____

Liked it?
circle one

Why? _____

Find some authentic candy from France at the pavilion. Try it. Did you notice the writing on the wrappers? What does the writing mean in your language? Keep the empty candy wrappers and attach them here.

29

copyright © 2016 D Magical Education. All Rights Reserved

UNITED KINGDOM

Patterned after the streets of London, the United Kingdom pavilion uses architecture to highlight styles of English buildings. These busy streets include a quaint pub, English cottage, tea shop, "fish and chips" eatery, and a medieval shop. At the end of the street, a real English garden complete with a hedge maze awaits!

UNITED KINGDOM
PAVILION OPENED
OCTOBER 1, 1982

ASK A KIDCOT CAST MEMBER TO WRITE YOUR NAME OR A SPECIAL MESSAGE (IN ENGLISH) IN THE BOX BELOW, THEN STAMP THE SMALLER SQUARE.

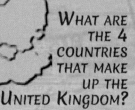

WHAT ARE THE 4 COUNTRIES THAT MAKE UP THE UNITED KINGDOM?

copyright © 2016 D Magical Education All Rights

United Kingdom UNITED KINGDOM

FLAG OF UNITED KINGDOM

CAPITAL	London
LANGUAGE	English
MONEY	Pound Sterling
PEOPLE	British, English, Scots, Irish, Welsh
CONTINENT	Europe

LIST YOUR 5 FAVORITE THINGS ABOUT THE UNITED KINGDOM PAVILION:

1. _____

2. _____

3. _____

4. _____

5. _____

copyright © 2016 D Magical Education. All Rights Reserved

UNITED KINGDOM

Find some authentic candy from the United Kingdom at the pavilion. Try it. Did you notice the writing on the wrappers? What does the writing mean in your language? Keep the empty candy wrappers and attach them here.

TRY 2 DIFFERENT FOODS FROM THE UNITED KINGDOM PAVILION. RATE HOW YOU LIKE THEM.

I tried: _____

Liked it?
circle one

Why? _____

I tried: _____

Liked it?
circle one

Why? _____

The outfits that each cast member wear, reflects their home country. How does the outfit for the United Kingdom pavilion cast members stand-out? If you need help, ask a cast member!

_____

_____

_____

_____

_____

copyright © 2016 D Magical Education All Rights

CANADA

The Canada pavilion is intended to share the great outdoors with its visitors. High above the gardens, the replica of the "Hotel du Canada" sets the backdrop against a replica Butchart Gardens of Victoria, full of waterfalls, fountains, and flowers. Don't miss the totem poles, reminders of Canada's Aboriginal peoples.

CANADA PAVILION OPENED OCTOBER 1, 1982

CAN YOU NAME THE 10 PROVINCES AND 3 TERRITORIES OF CANADA?

ASK A KIDCOT CAST MEMBER TO WRITE YOUR NAME OR A SPECIAL MESSAGE (IN ENGLISH) IN THE BOX BELOW, THEN STAMP THE SMALLER SQUARE.

copyright © 2016 D Magical Education. All Rights Reserved

CANADA

Canada

LIST YOUR 5 FAVORITE THINGS ABOUT THE CANADA PAVILION:

1. _____

2. _____

3. _____

4. _____

5. _____

FLAG OF CANADA

CAPITAL	Ottawa
LANGUAGE	English & French
MONEY	Canadian Dollar
PEOPLE	Canadians
CONTINENT	North America

copyright © 2016 D Magical Education All Rights

CANADA

The outfits that each cast member wear, reflects their home country. How does the outfit for the Canada pavilion cast members stand-out? If you need help, ask a cast member!

_____

_____

_____

_____

TRY 2 DIFFERENT FOODS FROM THE CANADA PAVILION. RATE HOW YOU LIKE THEM.

I tried: _____

Liked it?
circle one

Why? _____

I tried: _____

Liked it?
circle one

Why? _____

Find some authentic candy from Canada at the pavilion. Try it. Did you notice the writing on the wrappers? What does the writing mean in your language? Keep the empty candy wrappers and attach them here.

copyright © 2016 D Magical Education All Rights Reserved

PASSPORT TO THE WORLD

HAVE YOU VISITED ALL THE COUNTRIES AROUND "THE WORLD?"
USE THIS CHECKLIST TO MAKE SURE YOU SEE THEM ALL!

- ☐ MEXICO
- ☐ NORWAY
- ☐ CHINA
- ☐ GERMANY
- ☐ ITALY
- ☐ AMERICA
- ☐ JAPAN
- ☐ MOROCCO
- ☐ FRANCE
- ☐ UNITED KINGDOM
- ☐ CANADA

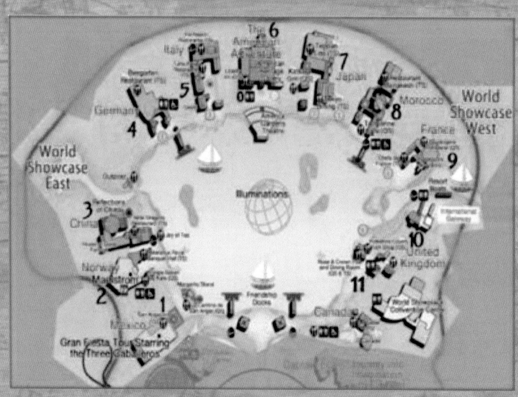

copyright © 2016 D Magical Education All Rights

Made in the USA
Monee, IL
04 January 2025

76054442R00024